Chickens Say What?

By J. L. Baumann

Printed in The United States of America
Link Printing, Groveland, Florida 34736

No part of this publication may be reproduced in whole or in part, or stored in a retrieval system, or transmitted in any form or by any means, electronic, mechanical, photocopying, recording, or otherwise, without written permission from the publisher. For information regarding permission, write to Post Mortem Publications, 146 East Broad Street, Groveland, FL 34736, or E-Mail: Contact@Postmortempublications.com

ISBN 978-1-941880-00-5

Copyright: ©Post Mortem Publications 2014
All rights reserved

Text by J.L. Baumann
Illustrations by Melodye Whitaker

~ First Edition ~

Fetchin's Farmers Market

Produce, Pullets, Pigs & Figs

- Naturally Local Vendors -

Range Rover Chickens
Meme's Goat Cheese
Beebe's Natural Honey
Herby's Healthy Herbs

Paula's Perky Peeps
Billy's Bio Beef
Vitality Vegetables
Farmington Fisheries

~ PLUS ~

A complete line of pulchritudinous Pork products from

"The Refined Swine"

The Exclusive Producers and Purveyors of the famous

REFINED SWINE PORK RINDS

~ Also Featuring ~

White's Meat Treats, *Arbuckle's Knuckles,* and Peck's Pickled Pig Feet

Visit our craft pavilion and food concession area
New vendors welcome • Fun for all • Bring the whole family

Four Corners Square, Downtown New Shoatly

Contents

Diginnity

This chicken pie's divine
The farmer said with relish
Plenty chicken stuffed inside
He continued to embellish

It's work to make the dough
His wife said with delight
You roll it out real slow
And pinch the edges tight

It's the chickens' work to eat
And that's the reason why
You also have to work
Or you shall have no pie

A Tisket, A Tasket

So I got up bright and early
When no one was around
Where is my Easter basket?
It was nowhere to be found

I think someone has hid it
For I dreamt it in my sleep
Who was the one who did it
The malo chickens peeped

The colored eggs were silent
As were all those jelly beans
And my basket was so vibrant
Filled up with nougat creams

It must have been the Bunny
There's no one else to blame
And his antics are not funny
The chocolate chicken claimed

Chicken Anyone?

The sky is going to fall
The chicken did proclaim
It will fall upon us all
Fat and skinny all the same

I must warn everyone
To get themselves prepared
For soon the day will come
And no one will be spared

The little chicken cried
And warned capriciously
If I'm going to end up fried
I'm going most deliciously

Eggsestentialism

I came first said the chicken
But the egg could not reply
With silence it was stricken
Too young to argue why

Then after chicken school
The egg now disavowed
Its thoughts as minuscule
Dismissed as unprofound

Attending Hen University
Must wiser she discovered
That life is not an adversity
It's a mystery to discover

Chicken Picken

Chicken and noodles, chicken and rice
Chicken with dumplings, is oh so nice
But Bar-B-Qued chicken is so succulent
Especially when smoked, it is excellent

Southern fried chicken is always a treat
And as you are thinking, it can't be beat
Along comes man with a different plan
With a roasted chicken in a baking pan

And what about all the choices of sides
The biscuits and gravy you cannot deny
It's corn on the cob, salted with butter
And after you eat it, you go for another

Oh so many choices, I just can't decide
I can't eat them all, God help me I tried

To Nestle

There was a little chickie
Who had the cutest peep
I knew it would be tricky
And certainly not cheap

I had to save my scratch
For I didn't want to beg
This relationship to hatch
And not just lay an egg

Alas, I built a lovely nest
Feathered soft with down
And feeling truly blessed
She finally stuck around

DANCE
CONTEST

LADIES FREE TONIGHT!

The Hunk of Funk

I tried the Funky Chicken
Cause I wanted to be cool
So I could have my pickin
Of all the chicks at school

I strutted and I bantered
As funky chickens do
So I could be the dancer
Admired by the brood

So I became impeccable
A classic piece of work
Unlike the other imbeciles
Who tried to do the Jerk

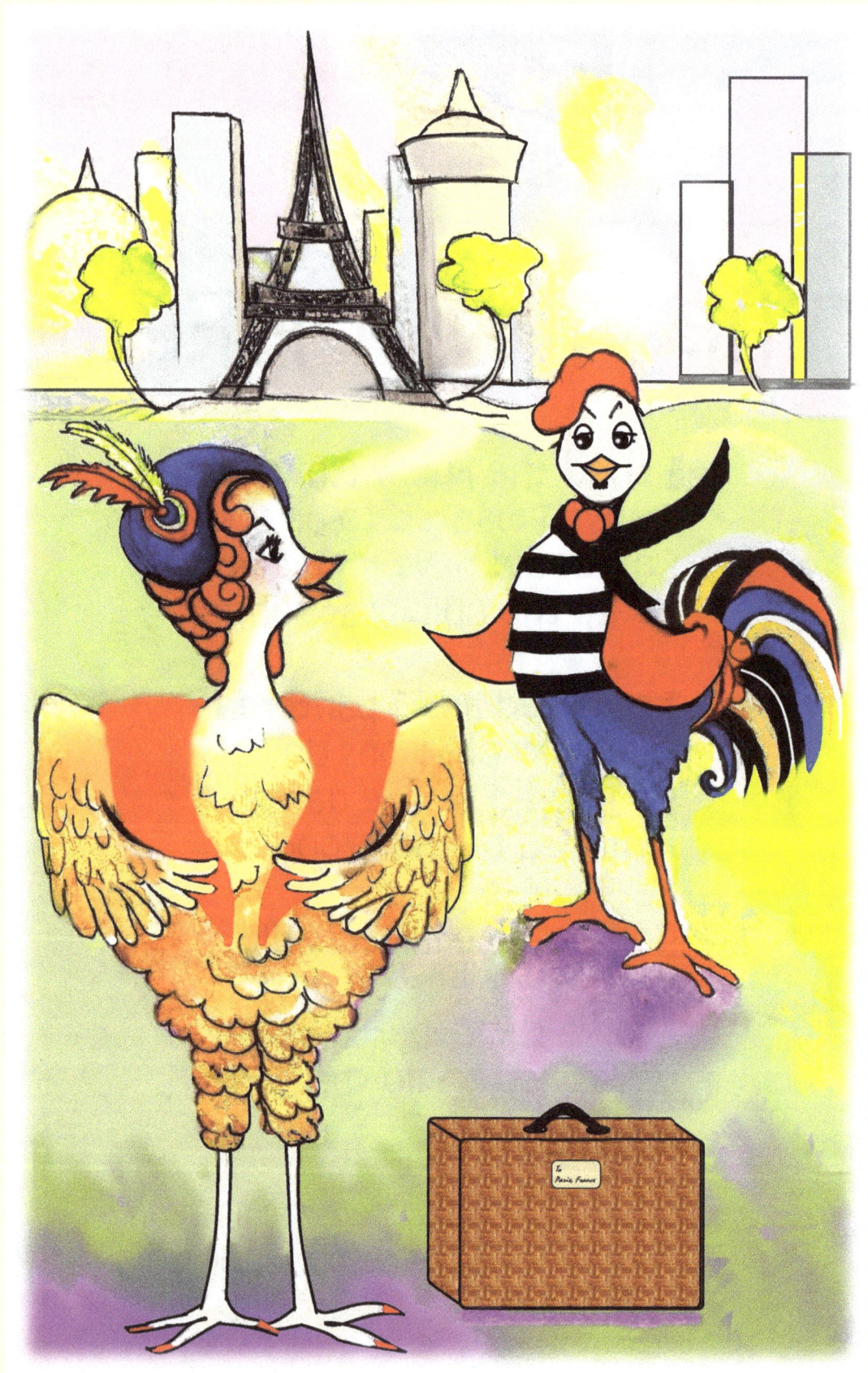

Fleedom

Cock a doodle do
The rooster called to me
What was I to do?
Surrender unequivocally

I'm a free range chicken
Not part of any flock
I roam to my convictions
His bantering's a crock

The chicken feed implored
To live in a chicken coop
Is something so abhorred
I'd rather be chicken soup

Souplexed

Chicken soup you need
To chase the cold away
And hardily I guarantee
I'll make it all the way

Egg noodles make it nice
And carrots give it flavor
As herbs will give it spice
A treat for you to savor

It's quite a healthy remedy
Whenever you are stricken
It's a cure for all humanity
But deadly to the chicken

Chicken Sense

Don't cross in the middle
Don't cross in the night
Don't cross as you fiddle
Don't cross in mid flight

Think now of your future
Think now of your past
Think now of the sutures
Think now of your task

You know of the chicken
You know of the street
You know time is tickin
You know of dead meat

L'eggalese

Hello my feathered friend
You need my help today?
It's the chickens I defend
Now let's discuss my pay

A chicken has its rights
I know the chicken laws
For you I'll dually fight
For scratch upon my paw

So the fox had guaranteed
She would perhaps survive
The nasty weasel's banditry
Surrendering her very pride

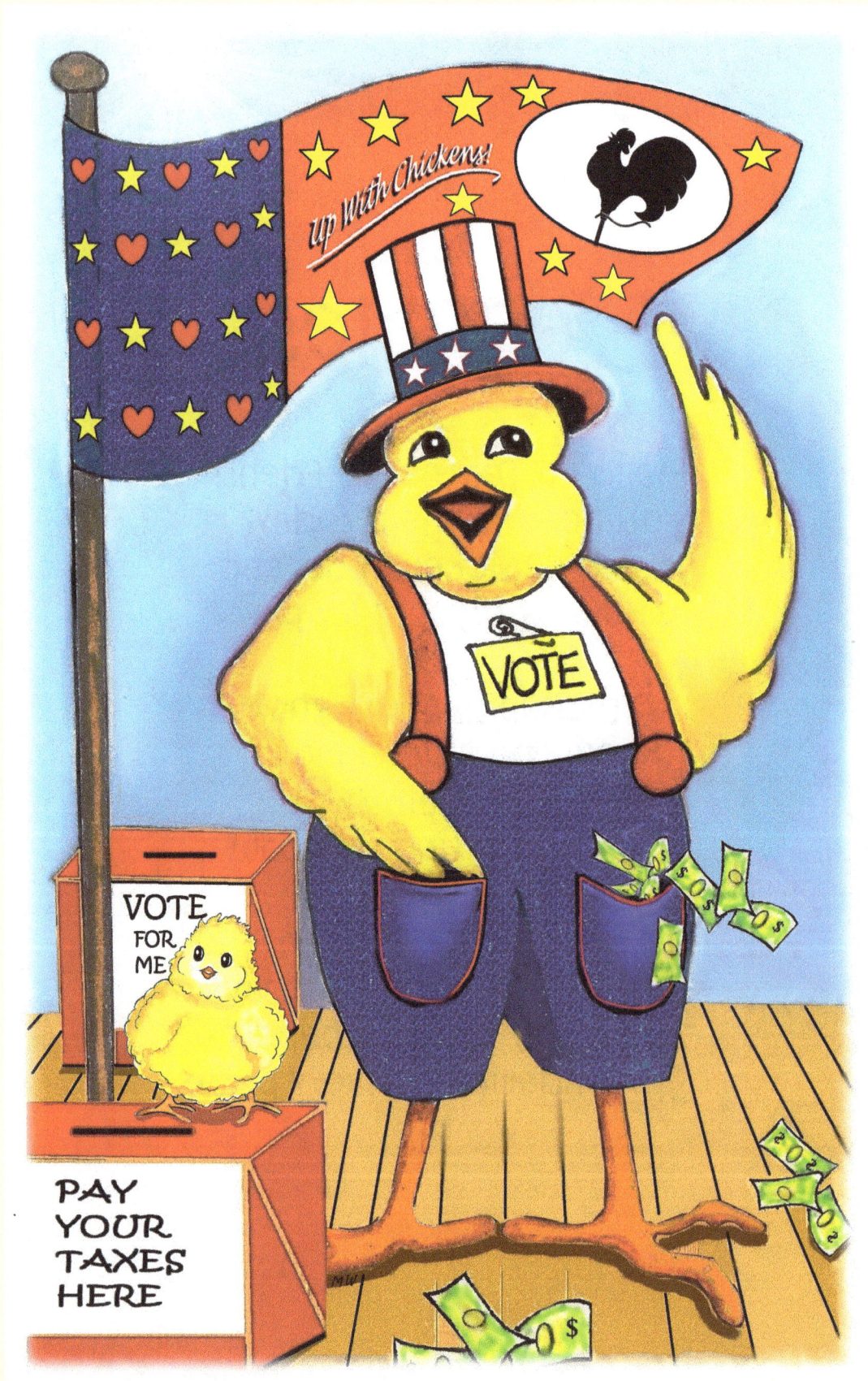

A Ringer

Up with the chickens
The politician cried
Cause time is atickin
On your vote I rely

For I need more tax
To pay all my friends
And you can relax
As my term extends

Pots full of chickens
I promise they'll be
So, some go akickin
-It won't affect me

Chicken Wired

So, I'm a people, the little chicken stated
No, you're a chicken, the old hen related
I'm free as a bird, the chick now declared
No, you're all fenced in, to know despair
Are people fenced in, asked the little bird?
All who are chicken, the old hen observed

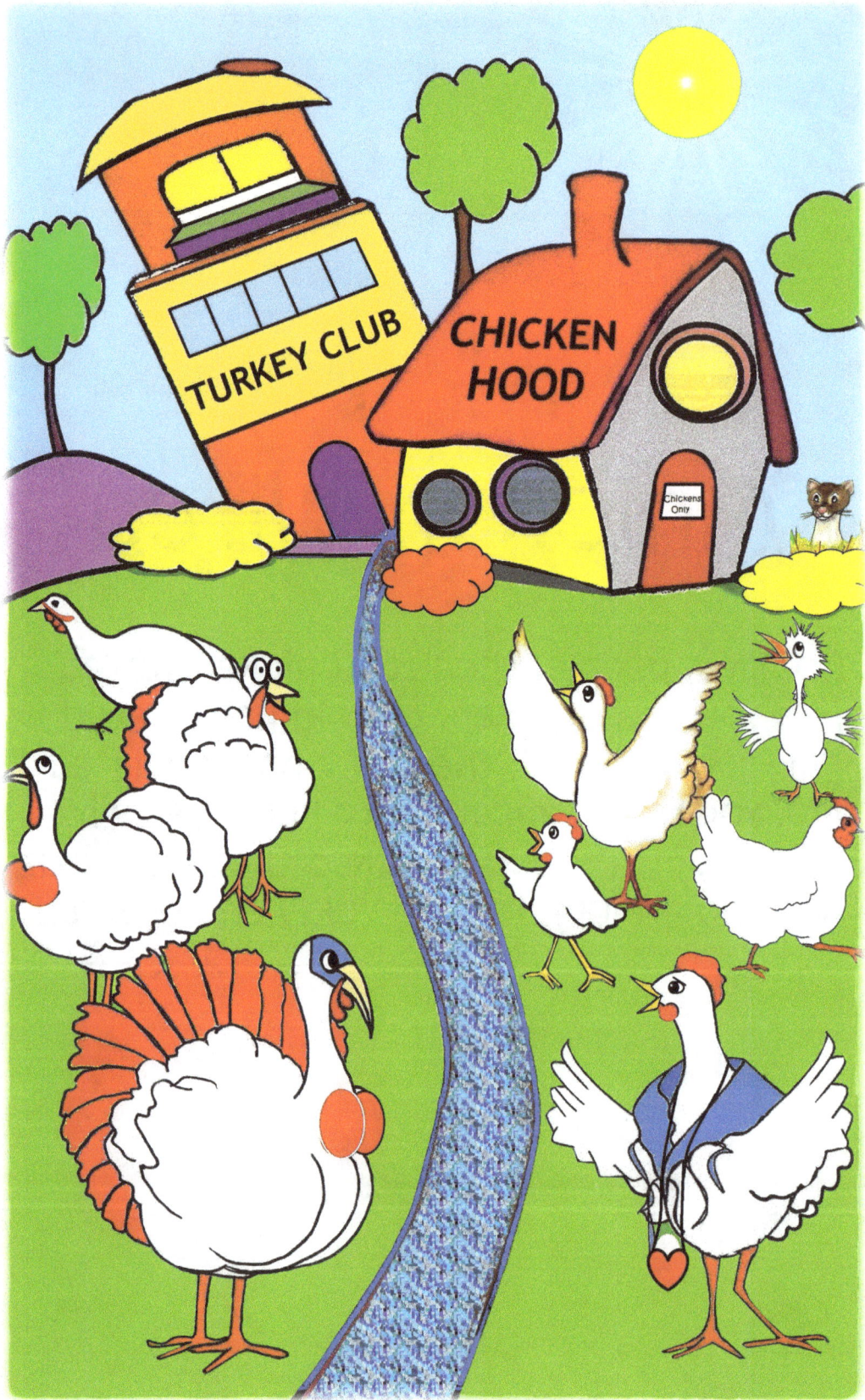

An Eggsoteric Eggschange

The chickens understood
There is safety in a flock
And created Chickenhood
To avoid a chicken crock

Turkeys weren't invited
Regarded to be dumb
The chickens all united
To vote them out as one

And so the Turkey Club
Refusing to be beaten
Reminded Chickenhood
Our eggs are never eaten

Professing Laureates

Eagles are imperious and taken oh so serious
But never want to play
Habitually oblivious, and never ever curious
Of laughter or dismay
So mysterious, and sometimes supercillious
With grandiose displays
Always so victorious, elegant while glorious
They're practically cliché

Chickens are industrious, and never bellicose
Day in, day out, they lay
Never taken serious and often quite hilarious
While roosters are risqué
Always quite notorious, reputedly inglorious
They never show dismay
Thankfully gregarious, giving Poet Laureates
Some humor to purvey

Chick n' Fat

I have to gain some weight
Clucked the big fat chicken
And I hope it's not too late
Tho I know that time's atickin

For the Rooster will come by
And I submit, I'll be prepared
To answer his beckon cry
And satisfy him without end

Spring chickens are delicious
And certainly, I'm not a fryer
So perhaps I'm not nutricious
But it's my fat he doth desire

Hen Pecked

The chickens clucked about
Pecking for a juicy worm
Pecking until all pecked out
Until it was confirmed

The worms had run away
Not wanting to be pecked
Clucking now in great dismay
What did they all expect?

The worms to just endure
A clucking chicken pecking
They'd rather find manure
And off they went a trekking

Fameininity

The egg was laid with joy
Laid in the nest with care
With happiness employed
But no one else was there

The hen did cackle loudly
The others ought to know
Again she cackled proudly
My egg's the best of show

She advertized her fame
To everyone ambitiously
And then the weasel came
And ate her egg deliciously

Kingly Duties

I'm no spring chicken
The old rooster said
Tho time is aticken
No way am I dead

I rise with the sun
To service the hens
And when I am done
I do it again

Cock-a-doodly-do
I cannot retire
This task I must do
For I am their Sire

To Run Afowl

The chickens ran around
Their little hearts apanic
A ticket had been found
For a ride on the Titanic

Perched high I saw it all
A rooster said with pride
It's curtains for you all
The trailer did decry

It's coming soon to you
It certainly conveyed
And nothing you can do
Can pray this fact away

"Firebrand" Chickens

Do chickens have a soul, the preacher asked his flock?
And know the end is near, as they're put inside a crock?
And so my feathered friends, what do you have to say?
I guess it all depends, did you confess your sins today?

Some chickens run away, quite terrified in mortal fear!
As I submit to you today, they knew the end was near!
Gorged to death on feed, they didn't say their prayers!
Then finally they understood, the meaning of prepared!

It's not about your dinner, with carrots, corn and peas!
It's boiling broth for you, whenever God ain't pleased!
And so the question really is, do chickens have a soul?
Are you prepared to testify, that chickens do not know?

So now you ask yourself, -do I have a soul of a chicken?
The Devil is prepared! -do you feel the flames a-lickin?

Deliverance

Her name was Cluckie
She was one of a kind
Her feathers all fluffy
With a buxom behind

Come up to my perch
She cackled one day
Now it ain't a church
So you need not pray

Of course I'll deliver
You don't need to beg
As then she bent over
And out came an egg

A Poem
Ode To The Chick
There was a little
Chickie,
Who had the
cutest peep,

Chicken?

I want to write a poem
The little chicken said
A poem to call my own
I can hear it in my head

I feel it would be great
If I can scratch it down
Thinking I can incubate
Some poetry profound

And so forever written
My poem was extolled
And all about a chicken
Who wanted to be bold

Faux Paw

A New York critic stated
That chickens cannot fly
I think that he was mated
With an alley cat nearby

Chickens aren't flightless
Like cats think in the city
But isn't he just priceless
He's a critic to be pittied

Chickens find him funny
Just pecking in the dirt
Pecking for some money
Not knowing he's a jerk

The Full Bull Fertilizer Co.

Believable, TX

For Crops or Cows Your Choice

- Propagation Brand Products
- How Now Cow Conceptions
- Majestic Meadow Muffins
- Max's Mature Manure

We Deliver Satisfaction

~ Sign Up For ~
'It's Nature's Way' Webinars
www.bulloneybenders.con

FRED & FANNIE'S FEED SUPPLY

Certified Dealers
of
Cow's Cud Brand
Dosey Doats Oats
Beak's Chicken Scratch

THEY NEED TO EAT, SO WE CAN!

Gluten, OK

Willie's Well Drilling
~ Have Rig, Will Dig ~

Pump Repair & Replacement

"We Drill Well"

Diggers, SC

Call THurston 5 - 8686

Cackle's Eggs

Home of
"The Big End First"
Premium Eggs

Let Us Lay Some On You!

Bedsprings, AR

Mammy's Country Cookbooks

*Mammy says -
Taint no better eatin' nowhere!*

~ Learn how to ~

**Bar-B-Que Bodaciously
Fry That Fresh Caught Fish
Cook Up Collards Quickly
&
Immortalize Your Grits**

Collect The Whole Set! Now Available On-Line!
www.mammy.mom

Seedling Brothers Nurseries

A Plethora of Pleasure

'Berry Delicious' Plants
Grandpa's Shoe Trees
Flora's Famous Bloomers
Rays's Radiant Bulbs

Call for Catalogue.....................1-800-HAY-SEED

The Hartland

Farm Supply Company

Quality, Quantity, and Quick Service

- **Chick N' Fat Fencing**
- **Ouchless Branding Irons**
- **Kickfree's Milking Stands**

If'n we ain't got it You cain't get it!

- **Forget Me Not Come-Alongs**
- **Barbie's "Prick-Free" Wire**
- **Woodchuck Brand Chainsaws**

A whole slew of locations - everywhere
Home Office - New York City, New York - Not!

Franchises Available

The Happy Tractor

New - Used & Aftermarket Parts

Visit Our 'You Pull Em' Graveyard All Makes and Models

Hard to find parts from the Nomo Tractor Company of Detroit, MI

Now Two Locations: Box Blade, IN and Harrow, CT

'Since 1912 - Till Forever'

www.ingramcontent.com/pod-product-compliance
Lightning Source LLC
Chambersburg PA
CBHW080528110426
42742CB00017B/3272